INDIA
Land, Life and Culture

Plants and Agriculture

ROSEMARY SACHDEV

MACMILLAN
LIBRARY

First published in 2009 by
MACMILLAN EDUCATION AUSTRALIA PTY LTD
15–19 Claremont Street, South Yarra 3141

Visit our website at www.macmillan.com.au or go directly to www.macmillanlibrary.com.au

Associated companies and representatives throughout the world.

National Library of Australia Cataloguing-in-Publication data

Sachdev, Rosemary.
    Plants and agriculture / Rosemary Sachdev.

    ISBN 978 1 4202 6713 6
    Sachdev, Rosemary. India: Land, life and culture.
    Includes index.
    For primary school age.
    Plants – India – Juvenile literature. Agriculture – India – Juvenile literature.
954

Edited by Kath Kovac
Text and cover design by Peter Shaw
Page layout by Kerri Wilson
Photo research by Lesya Bryndzia
Illustrations by Damien Demaj, DEMAP

Printed in China

Acknowledgements

Dedicated to Jasbir, who gave me India, and to Arkin, Amaya and Naira who belong and who will read these books some day.

With special thanks to the Archaeological Survey of India in New Delhi and Aurangabad for permission to take photographs in the Ajanta Caves with a camera and tripod, and thanks to the National Museum of India, Janpath, New Delhi for permission to photograph replicas in the Museum shop. Lastly, many thanks to La Boutique, Sunder Nagar, New Delhi, for the photograph of their joint family and their help in allowing us to photograph prints, paintings and artefacts from their collection.

With many thanks to all those who gave time for photographs and interviews, for lending their children to be photographed and for helping in the many ways they did and especial thanks to Jatinder, without whose tireless travel and wonderful photographs, these books would never have happened.

The author and the publisher are grateful to the following for permission to reproduce copyright material:

All photographs courtesy of Jatinder Marwaha except for:
Collection of RJ Sachdev, **29** (right); RJ Sachdev, **6** (bottom left), **14** (all), **18** (right, second right), **19** (top), **20** (top), **21** (bottom); SNEHIT/Shutterstock, **6** (top); Wikipedia/Pollinator, **28** (top).

While every care has been taken to trace and acknowledge copyright, the publisher tenders their apologies for any accidental infringement where copyright has proved untraceable. Where the attempt has been unsuccessful, the publisher welcomes information that would redress the situation.

K2
8611 m

Karakoram Range

*Kashmir
Valley*

Ladakh Range

Indus

River

A S I A

H I M A L A Y A S

Kanchenjunga ▲
8598 m

River

Sutlej

River

Indus

T h a r   D e s e r t

Yamuna

Ganga

(Ganges)

G a n g e t i c   P l a i n

River

Chambal

River

River

Betwa

*Ganga
(Ganges)*

River

Brahmaputra   *River*

Rann of Kutch

f of Kutch

Vindhya Ranges

River

Satpura Ranges

Narmada

River

Tapi

Gulf of Khambhat

Penganga

River

Tropic of Cancer

Sundarbans Delta

Mahanadi   River

Hooghly River

Bay of Bengal

Godavari

**DECCAN
PLATEAU**

River

E a s t e r n   G h a t s

W e s t e r n   G h a t s

Krishna

River

*Arabian
Sea*

Penneru

River

M a l a b a r   C o a s t

Kaveri

**Nilgiri
Hills**

River

*Andaman
Islands*

**Lakashadweep
Islands**

C o r o m a n d e l   C o a s t

Cardamom Hills

Palk Strait

N

*Andaman
Sea*

*Nicobar
Islands*

*Gulf of
Mannar*

**Cape
Comorin**

INDIAN OCEAN

Key
Height in metres (m)

0–200

200–500

500–1000

1000–4000

4000 and above

0   300   600   900 kilometres

Scale

Contents

Showing respect

Indian people always use titles with people's names to be polite, such as Shri and Shrimati if speaking Hindi, the national language, or Mr and Mrs if speaking English. These titles are different all over India, and their form depends on the family relationship or the seniority of the person addressed.

Glossary Words

When a word is printed in **bold**, you can look up its meaning in the Glossary on page 31.

India, a land of diversity

India is a land of great **diversity**, which can be seen in its arts, culture, people, landscape and climates. For every description of Indian life, there are many different but equally true variations.

India has a very long history. People have lived in India for around 10 000 years and come from many different racial backgrounds. They speak hundreds of languages; some spoken by millions of Indians, others spoken by only a few thousand. The country has many different landscapes and climates, from freezing mountains to hot, tropical areas.

India came under British influence in the 1600s, and Britain took control of India in the 1850s. India gained its independence from Britain in 1947 and became a **republic** in 1950.

Ancient carvings

Mountainous landscapes

Majestic tombs

Many religions

Unique plants

Wild animals

This book explains how India's many different climatic regions and temperature variations allow a huge variety of plants to grow. Many plants are seasonal, but at some time, somewhere, all the plants of the world could be grown in India.

Diversity of plants

India's wide range of climates allows a huge variety of plant life to grow. The vegetation changes from tropical rainforests in the south to mountainous alpine forests in the cold north.

India's deserts in the west and coastal regions in the west and east also have their own types of vegetation, such as thorny trees and large evergreen trees.

Every different area of India has its own varieties of trees, shrubs and flowers. Crops of all kinds are grown, both for food and commercial use, such as rubber production.

Marigolds are used in many religious festivals.

Fruit and vegetables of all types are grown across the country. Some of these grow all year, and others can only be grown during certain seasons of the year. Other varieties of fruit and vegetables have only recently been introduced into India from other countries.

People have experimented with growing different foods in different climates. Somewhere in India, a suitable climate is found for every type of seed.

Oranges come in different varieties for juicing or eating, and the most popular eating variety is the santra.

Vegetables are often sold in wholesale markets.

Forests

Every type of forest in the world grows in India. The type of forest that grows in a particular area depends on that region's climate and **altitude**.

Tropical rainforests

Tropical rainforests grow on the south-west coast of India. Some of the world's richest evergreen trees grow here. Rosewood, ebony and mahogany trees are used to make furniture and wooden handicrafts such as toys, household items and sculptures.

For Your Information

Rosewood has red wood, ebony wood is black and mahogany wood is a deep brown.

Tropical rainforest trees grow in warm, humid regions.

Pine trees such as these are used for building and to make packing boxes.

Deciduous forests

Throughout most of India, many trees shed their leaves at the end of winter. The new leaves grow as the old leaves are falling, so the trees are never completely bare. The wood of teak, shisham and sal trees is used for building purposes and making furniture.

Mountain forests

In the lower mountains, at altitudes of about 3000 metres, evergreen pine and fir trees with long spiky leaves are common. Deciduous cedar and deodar trees, used for building and furniture, grow in the hills above 1000 metres.

Thorny trees

Some of India's most common trees are thorny and scrubby. The thorny kikar tree is found everywhere. It makes a useful living hedge, as it can grow anywhere with very little care. An acacia tree, sometimes called khair, also grows in many areas. Khair is a source of gum and a type of varnish called shellac, and its wood and charcoal are used as fuel.

Thorny forests are common in India, as these trees don't need much water to survive.

Bamboo is a tall grass that can grow in most areas of India but grows wild in the north-east.

Mangroves

Mangrove trees are specially adapted to grow in salty water. Mangrove swamps are found on the west coast and in the **delta** region of the east. They protect the coast from erosion damage and protect the land from hurricanes and **tsunamis**.

Mangroves commonly grow in the water in hot areas of the coast and deltas.

For Your Information

One special type of bamboo flowers only once about every 50 years. The last time it flowered was in 2007. Small animals, such as rats, love the fruit of this bamboo and will come from different regions to find it. They grow fat eating not only the bamboo, but all the other crops in the area. If the animals are not controlled, this can cause **famine**.

India's trees

Some of India's trees are unusual, have religious associations or are very old and large.

Banyan tree

The roots of the banyan tree grow from its branches as well as in the ground. These 'aerial' roots grow downwards until they reach the ground and can soak up **nutrients** from the soil.

This banyan tree growing in Kolkata, West Bengal, is more than 100 years old and is 500 metres in circumference.

Peepul trees can grow anywhere from seed.

Peepul tree

The peepul tree is considered holy by Hindus and Buddhists. It is said that the Buddha sat under a peepul tree while he meditated to gain enlightenment. Peepul trees can be a nuisance as they can grow in cracks in walls and on terraces. It is almost impossible to get rid of them.

A small **shrine** to a Hindu god will often be found under a peepul tree.

For Your Information

Sandalwood trees, which grow in the south of India, have a lovely smell when the wood is cut. Sandalwood was once used for making large boxes, but it is now less available, so it is used for making small boxes or images of gods.

Flowering trees

India is famous for its colourful, flowering trees. Many of them start to flower in the very short spring and some keep flowering right through the hot summer.

The rhododendron tree is covered with bright red flowers for a short time each year. In the hill regions of north India, it grows very tall. When the British took rhododendrons to England, however, they never grew very large and only ever looked like shrubs.

India's flowering trees

The gul mohur tree is very large and is the best-known of the many red-flowering trees in India. It flowers right through the summer.

The amaltas is a small, flowering tree that has long, drooping bunches of yellow flowers in early summer.

The seed pods that develop after the red flowers of the silk cotton tree fall are full of a very soft material used for stuffing pillows, cushions and quilts.

Spices

Most of the world's spices are grown and used in India, although only a few spices originally came from India.

Pepper

Pepper is native to India and comes from the south-western **Ghats**. The plants need a hot and humid climate and grow from ground at sea level to ground at heights of 1500 metres. The first traders from Europe came to India for pepper, which they used to flavour meat that had started to decay during their long winters.

Turmeric

Turmeric is a yellow powder that comes from the **rhizomes** of the turmeric plant. It is added to food during cooking to give extra flavour and a yellow colour. It is the main ingredient of curry powder, which can be used when cooking Indian food.

For Your Information

Pepper vines are grown against wooden tree poles. The vines' clinging roots help it hold onto the pole for support.

Peppercorns are the berry of the pepper vine, and they are green when growing, ripen to red and dry to black.

Whole turmeric rhizomes are boiled, dried, cleaned and polished before being ground into powder.

Did You Know?

Curry leaves are the small, dark green leaves of a tree that grows throughout India. They add a delicate flavour to some dishes and are most commonly used in southern India.

Coriander

Dry, ground coriander seeds are one of the main spices used in Indian cooking. The chopped green leaves are also sprinkled on some dishes before they are served.

Tejpat

Tejpat leaves are usually called bay leaves, although they come from the cassia tree. They taste like cloves and smell a bit like pepper. The trees grow in hot, humid areas of the Himalayas.

Tamarind

Tamarind trees produce long, wrinkled pods with brittle skin. The pods are full of brown seeds in a sticky white pulp that has a sweet, sour and spicy taste.

Many different types of spices are bought and sold at the spice market.

Tamarind, shown here drying in the sun, originally came from Africa, but is grown widely in India.

MEET Lalasab

Lalasab is a spice seller who lives in Hubli, Karnataka. He buys spices wholesale in big bags and then sells them in small amounts for people's household cooking use. He works 12 hours a day.

In conversation with Lalasab

I didn't get to study very much, because I had to work on the family farm. I have two children, a boy that is two months old and girl that is three years old, and I want a better life for them.

11

Chillies

Chillies are used to give the hot taste that is usual in Indian food.

The chilli plant originally came from South America. Chillies grow on small bushes and start off green, then ripen to red. Green ones are used fresh in cooking, but are also often eaten raw. Red chillies are dried and used whole or ground into powder.

Did You Know?

Many Indian people eat hot green or red chillies whole.

Chillies act as a preservative, which is essential in a hot country such as India, where most people do not have refrigerators.

Imported spices

Many of the spices used in Indian cooking, such as cloves, cardamom and nutmeg, were originally brought from the Spice Islands, now part of Indonesia. They only grow in the south-western state of Kerala, where the climate is suitable. Spices have been traded along Kerala's long sea coast for hundreds of years.

Garam masala is a spice mix that contains ground cloves, cinnamon, cumin, large and small cardamom, star anise, mace and nutmeg.

Medicinal plants

India has a very old system of medicine, called Ayurveda, which is based on the healing properties of certain plants. Ayurveda is still practiced by some specially trained doctors.

Neem

The neem tree is one of the most useful trees in India. The smell of the leaves keeps away pests such as moths and mosquitoes. Neem leaves are also soaked in water and used as a healing bath for wounds and burns.

Tulsi

Also called holy basil, the tulsi plant is worshipped as a sacred plant throughout India. It is grown in pots in the gardens and courtyards of many Indian houses. The oil in its leaves repels mosquitoes and flies.

For Your Information

Tulsi leaves can be used to make a tea that soothes coughs. Powdered tulsi leaves added to dried ginger and sugar in hot water reduces fever, and the boiled juice cures many skin problems. The leaves can also be eaten to treat a cold or sore throat.

Amla

The fruit of the amla tree, which is a rich source of Vitamin C, helps people to digest food. Dried amla boosts the immune system and also brings down fever.

Every part of the neem tree, from the leaves to the bark, has a useful purpose.

Indian scientists are trying to find a cure for cancer with the tulsi plant.

13

Staple foods

Wheat and rice are India's staple foods. Indians eat them with every meal, just as many Australians eat potatoes and Italians eat pasta.

Wheat

In general, north Indians eat wheat, and everyone else eats rice. Families in the north serve freshly made wholewheat flat breads, or **rotis**, called **chapatis**.

In the desert regions of the west, flour from grains such as maize, millet and sorghum is also used to make rotis.

Growing and harvesting wheat

Wheat is grown in the north and central areas of India. It is sometimes cut by hand and sometimes by machine, depending on the size of the farm and the wealth of the farmer.

Did You Know?

'Double roti' is western-style bread cooked in a conventional oven. It is not normally made fresh at home like the flat rotis are.

Flour from wheat such as this is used to make roti.

Wheat is planted in January in the same fields that rice was grown in the year before, and is harvested in April.

Rice

Rice used to be grown everywhere in India, except in the desert and the wheat-growing areas of the north. Now, irrigation has meant that rice can also be grown in the north.

Growing rice

Planting rice is very hard work. The fields have to be flooded from canals or wells. Once they are covered in water, the fields are ploughed and the rice seeds are planted. After the rice seedlings have grown to a height of a few centimetres, they are replanted in rows, one seedling at a time.

The ground has to be kept wet or the rice will not grow, so there must be plenty of water near the fields. Once the rice is ready for harvest, it is cut, usually by hand.

Types of rice

Rice comes in different qualities. The name of India's special long-grain rice, 'basmati', has been patented, which means no other country can call rice by this name. Basmati is the most expensive rice and, when cooked properly, each grain is separate. Other cheaper rice has short grains that tend to stick together.

Different rice grains include basmati, parmal, brown and broken basmati, which is cheaper than normal basmati.

After rice plants have flowered, the grains take about three months to ripen.

Sugar and edible oils

Sugar cane has been grown and used to make sugar in India for 2500 years. Sugar cane plants take almost a year to grow, and are grown almost all through India. The sugar cane is sent to a mill, where it is crushed to release the cane juice. Sugar is produced from the juice, then processed and sent to the markets.

All Indian food is cooked in oil or ghee. Different oils are used depending on what grows better in a region. Peanut, coconut, mustard, safflower, sunflower and corn oil are all produced in India.

Oil seeds are crushed by machines and used in cooking.

Did You Know?

India is the second-largest producer of sugar cane and edible oils in the world.

Kesar Singh crushes tough sugar cane stalks with a machine.

MEET Kesar Singh

Kesar Singh is a sugar cane juice seller who lives a village near Udaipur in Rajasthan. He has been selling juice for 15 years. For the first few years, he rented a machine, but he now owns one. He buys sugar cane from the wholesale vegetable market.

In conversation with Kesar Singh

I sell about 15 to 20 glasses at three rupees per glass in the winter, but up to 125 glasses a day in the summer.

There is no functioning school near our village so my children cannot study. I hope to improve my life and give my children a better chance.

Tea and coffee

Although tea and coffee are very important crops in India, they are only grown in small areas with the right climate. Tea grows in the low north eastern and southern hills, and coffee grows in the southern hills.

Tea production

Only the very top, new leaves of tea shrubs are picked, as these have the most delicate taste after they are dried and cut into pieces. Cheaper teas are made from small pieces of leftover leaves.

Many tea stalls can be found at roadsides throughout India.

Tea needs a wet climate with mild temperatures.

MEET Bunnu Bishokarma

Bunnu Bishokarma is a tea-picker at a tea estate in Darjeeling. She has been working for the past 20 years, usually from February to December, from 7.30 a.m. to 3.00 p.m.

In conversation with Bunnu Bishokarma

Only women work as tea-pickers because we are more careful with the leaves, picking only those which are ready each morning. In this area there are very few jobs and my three grown sons and my husband are unemployed.

Coffee production

Coffee is drunk in the south, but in most other areas it is considered a luxury. Coffee beans are picked and dried when they turn red. The bean then becomes brown and its outer skin is removed. The inner part is processed to make coffee.

Vegetables

Many Indians are vegetarians, so people eat a wide range of vegetables and have many ways of cooking them. All vegetables are cooked with spices. Vegetable names vary in different states of India, so only English names are given here.

Basic vegetables

Onions and tomatoes are used in almost all Indian cooking. The Indian onion has a brittle red–purple skin and is white inside with light purple rings. It is not strong tasting and can be eaten raw. Chopped onion is usually the first thing to be put into food to be cooked. Tomatoes are expensive, but may also be used with onions as the base of cooked food.

Pods of garlic are commonly used in Indian cooking, crushed or whole. Ginger is also used, as a paste or cut into small pieces.

Common vegetables

The sweet potato has been used in India for many centuries. The common potato was introduced by the Portuguese in the 1500s. Yams are a commonly eaten vegetable in the south. Pumpkin, marrow, cucumber, peas and beans are always available.

Commonly used vegetables in India

Garlic

Ginger

Onions

Tomatoes

Leafy vegetables

Indians grow cauliflower, cabbage and spinach, as well as native leafy vegetables. Fenugreek has small, green leaves and a strong taste. Amaranth, which is like a red-leafed spinach, is popular in the south, and mustard leaf is grown in the north.

Root vegetables

The white Indian radish grows up to 30 centimetres long and hundreds are sold in the vegetable market, or 'sabzi mandi'.

Beetroot is often eaten raw in India, instead of cooked. The white Indian radish has been used in India for thousands of years. Indian carrots come in many different colours, from yellow, orange and red to dark red and almost black.

The black carrot grows in the north in winter, and is used to make a popular drink called kanji.

Okra

Okra is a green pod about 10 centimetres long. It can be cooked in small pieces or stuffed with spices and fried whole.

Okra is also called lady's finger because of its long, slender shape.

Did You Know?

In winter, carrots are made into a delicious sweet dish called gajar ka halwa. They are grated and cooked for many hours in milk, often with sliced almonds and sultanas added. The gajar ka halwa is eaten hot.

Special vegetables

India has some unusual vegetables that are not often seen in other countries.

Water chestnut

The water chestnut grows under water. The root is eaten boiled and spiced. It is also ground into flour and used during some religious festivals when grain is forbidden.

Lotus root

The lotus also grows in water. The root is a long cylinder that is picked from the water when ripe, and chopped and cooked with spices, particularly in Kashmir.

Water chestnut roots are harvested after the monsoon is over.

MEET Madhav Sahakari

Madhav Sahakari is an **organic** farmer. The farm is owned by four brothers and has been in the family since 1842.

In conversation with Madhav Sahakari

We went fully organic in 1983 and times were hard until 1997. Now, people know the impact of chemicals on our environment and many are more willing to buy the slightly more expensive organic foods. For us, the decision was partly economic and partly social. The earlier method, using pesticides and fertilisers, used less labour. We could only hire labour for two weeks, which was not good for them or for us. They would often move away to other jobs. We turned to labour-intensive organic farming, so our workers have more security and we have lower capital costs.

The drumstick is used in many south Indian dishes.

Jackfruit has been grown in India for more than 3000 years.

Drumstick

The drumstick looks like a long green stick. It is full of fibre and its flesh has to be sucked out of the cooked vegetable.

Jackfruit

Jackfruit is eaten as a vegetable before it is ripe, when it used as a meat substitute, because it has a similar texture to meat. When ripe, it is eaten as a fruit, and has a sweeter flavour.

Eggplant

Eggplant is native to India. Large, round, purple eggplants are grilled until the skin cracks and peels off. The flesh is then cooked. Small white or purple eggplants can be stuffed with spices and fried whole. Long, thin, purple eggplants are chopped and cooked.

Eggplants come in different sizes, shapes and colours.

For Your Information

Mushrooms became popular in India around 1995, when button mushrooms started being grown commercially. Kashmiri people, however, have been growing mushrooms for years. The large guchi, marel and dhengi varieties are dried, packed, and sold to the rest of India.

Pulses

As so many Indians are either vegetarian or too poor to buy meat, they get most of their **protein** from pulses, or lentils, which are different varieties of dried peas and beans. Every meal will include some form of cooked lentils, as well as vegetables. They can be used whole or split, and many need to be soaked overnight before cooking. This reduces cooking time and gets rid of toxins.

This lady is cooking a kidney bean dish for her family.

Peas and beans

The chick pea, which can be light or dark brown, is one of the larger pulses. Before being dried, the green chick pea is eaten as a vegetable for a short season in the northern winter.

Brown-coloured black-eyed beans are small and take less time to cook than larger red kidney beans.

Dried beans come in dark red, light red and speckled red varieties, and may be served with rice after cooking. They are a favourite with children.

Daals

Some lentils resemble small peas. When they are split, they are called daals.

There are more than twelve types of daals in India. They can be cooked as a thick, almost solid, liquid, or as a slightly thinner liquid with vegetables, such as sambhar. They can also be cooked as a thin, clear soup called rasam.

Daals have soft outer cases and can be white, brown, pink, green or yellow before cooking. As turmeric is usually added to daals when cooking, many turn yellow by the time they are ready for eating.

This shop sells a wide variety of daal.

Lentil snacks

Lentil flour can be used to make many snacks. **Idli** and **dosa** are snacks found in the south, and **dhokla** and **khanvi** are snacks common in the west.

Adding lentils to snacks in a country where so many people are vegetarian is useful as they provide protein, which is necessary for a healthy diet.

Types of daal

Whole masoor daal

Whole moong daal

Whole urad daal

Split masoor daal

Split moong daal

Split urad daal

Fruits

These days, most fruits are available in Indian cities. Until imports were allowed recently, only locally grown fruits could be bought, and most of these have a very short season, or time when they are ready to eat.

Mangoes

Indian mangoes are famous around the world. There are many varieties which grow all over the north as well as in coastal areas. The most popular variety of mango is the alphonso, from Goa on the west coast.

Mangoes are roughly oval in shape, but have one pointed end. They have one very large seed. Each mango hangs from a single long stalk on a large, shady tree.

Mangoes are green before they ripen. Ripe mangoes may have green, red or yellow skin depending on the variety. The fleshy part of the fruit is yellow or orange.

Types of mangoes

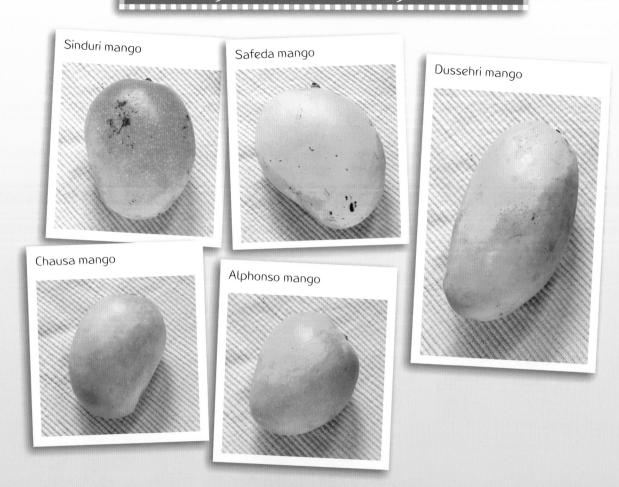

Sinduri mango

Safeda mango

Dussehri mango

Chausa mango

Alphonso mango

Papayas

Papayas are soft fruits with yellow or green skin and yellow or orange flesh. They can vary in size from ten centimetres to more than 30 centimetres long. Papayas grow throughout India all year long.

Melons

There are many varieties of melons in India. Melons grow in dry riverbeds and ripen in summer after a short growing season. Once the monsoon comes and the rivers fill, the melon season is over.

Oranges

Different varieties of oranges grow in India. The most popular eating variety is the santra, which has a loose skin and is about six centimetres across. Other varieties, which are usually juiced, are the malta, the mausambi and the kinoo.

Litchis

Litchis have a hard, red skin when ripe. They open easily and have firm, white flesh surrounding a brown oval-shaped seed.

Bananas are sold in bunches in wholesale markets, where they are popular and cheap.

Litchis originally came from China and have a very short growing season.

25

Flowers

India does not have very many native flowers. Most of its flowers were brought to India by the Mughals and the Europeans. There is a growing export market for flowers that can grow in the north Indian winter, when it is too cold in Europe and America.

This red lotus flower is growing in a pool in Delhi.

Native flowers

The red lotus is India's national flower. It appears in many traditional and religious paintings. Other native flowers are blue and white waterlilies, musk rose, lilies, and the blue poppy and wild tulip of Kashmir.

Marigolds

Marigolds are the most commonly seen flower in India. They grow and flower the whole year. Travellers are often given marigold garlands upon arrival as a gesture of welcome. All happy festivals or ceremonies use marigolds as decoration or as part of the ceremony.

Marigold flowers and garlands are used at weddings and festivals, and on religious occasions.

MEET Prem Kumar

Prem Kumar is a flower-seller outside Jaisalmer Fort in Rajasthan. He sells flowers, mostly marigolds, at his stall outside the fort's main gate from 6.00 a.m. till 9.00 p.m. Visitors to temples in and around the fort buy the flowers as offerings. The flowers come by truck from wholesalers in Jodhpur. He buys about 10 kilograms per day and about 20 kilograms on festival days.

Jasmine

The jasmine is a creeper with a small, white flower. It is used in religious festivals and is also made into small garlands that many Indian women wear in their hair.

The champa tree's white flowers have a very sweet smell.

Girls often wear flower garlands in their hair.

Orchids

Orchids are native to India, but have been taken to so many other parts of the world that this is generally not known. Orchids still grow naturally in India's hilly areas, mostly in the north-east.

More than 60 different varieties of orchids are found in India. Some have very interesting names that try to describe the flower's appearance. Some of these are the butterfly orchid, lady's slipper orchid, dancing lady orchid, fox brush orchid and monkey orchid.

Orchids from the northern state of Sikkim are brought to Delhi shops to be sold as exotic flowers.

27

Nuts

India has a variety of nuts but most are expensive and not many Indians can afford them.

Peanuts

Peanuts are pressed for oil or eaten as a snack. They can be roasted, salted, dipped in spices, fried or eaten raw.

Peanuts are also added to toffee. The toffee is cooled and cut into squares, as with peanut brittle.

Peanuts grow under the ground in bunches that sprout from the roots.

For Your Information

Almonds are believed to be very good for the brain. Indian children are given almonds to eat before they sit for exams.

Cashews

Cashew nuts hang from the fruit of the cashew nut tree. Most of the fruit of the cashew nut tree is fed to cattle, but some is used to make a fermented drink, called feni, after the nut is removed.

Cashew nuts are eaten salted, dipped in spices, fried or raw.

MEET Krishna Gowde

Krishna Gowde is a spice plantation worker who lives in a village near Goa. He has been working since he was 14.

In conversation with Krishna Gowde

I attend to the cashew trees on the farm. We clear the area around the cashew tree in November and it is ready with fruit by March or April. The ripe fruit falls to the ground and we separate the hard shelled nut at the base of the fruit. The fruit is crushed and the juice fermented. The nut is sent to the cashew factories for processing.

Cash crops

India grows many very important non-food cash crops that are sold for commercial purposes.

Cotton

Cotton has been grown in India for thousands of years. When supplies of cotton from America stopped due to the American Civil War (1861–1865), the British government made Indians grow even more cotton. The raw cotton was sent back to Britain, where it was spun and woven into cloth by machine and sold back to India at a high price.

Did You Know?

Calico, a type of cloth made from cotton, comes from the town of Calicut, in the state of Kerala.

Rubber

Rubber tree plantations can be found in Kerala and some north-eastern states. The sticky, white sap runs down a groove cut in the tree's trunk and into a fixed container. Collecting the rubber sap is called tapping. The sap is sent to a factory for processing into sheets of raw rubber, which are used for car tyres and tubes.

Jute, a crop grown in the eastern region of India, is used to make hessian sacks.

Cotton is taken to market, where it will be sold, then spun into yarn, and later woven into cloth.

For Your Information

The flax plant is used for making an expensive fabric called linen, as well as linseed oil, which is used to make paint.

Mughal gardens

The Mughal emperor, Babur, conquered the rulers of India in 1526. He came from a fairly barren area of Central Asia. His people built gardens to create green areas in the desert regions where they lived before coming to India.

Garden design

Mughal gardens are laid out in geometric patterns with an emphasis on water and fountains. They have paved areas and walks, grass, water pools and fountains, trees and flowers. Most of the gardens have a building in the middle.

Kashmir gardens

In Kashmir, where the climate is much cooler, it is easier to grow a variety of flowers and trees. The Mughal emperors liked to spend their summers in Kashmir, and built many gardens there with water pools and fountains. These gardens are still popular today with Kashmiris and tourists.

For Your Information

When Babur first arrived in India, he commented on the lack of good fruit and flowers. He knew he had to create gardens to grow the fruit he wanted, and so he and his descendants created gardens in all the areas they controlled.

Kashmir has many Mughal gardens, which are rather bare in winter but still popular.

This Mughal garden lies in front of the Taj Mahal, and is seen here with the entrance gate in the background.

Glossary

altitude	height above sea level
chapatis	Indian breads of wholemeal flour cooked on a metal griddle over a fire
delta	flat land, usually triangular in shape, through which a river takes many paths to the sea
dhokla	a mixture of ground daal and chick pea flour, steamed and cut into squares
diversity	great variety
dosa	a large, thin pancake made from rice flour and ground daal
famine	a very bad shortage of food or water in a district
Ghats	the range of low hills running down the east and west coast of India
idli	a steamed patty made from rice flour and ground daal
khanvi	a snack made from a mixture of ground daal and chick pea flour, rolled into a cylinder shape
nutrients	substances or chemical compounds needed for growth
organic	vegetables grown without using any chemical fertilisers or pesticides
protein	a compound in food that is very important for health
republic	a form of government where the rulers are elected by the people and the leader is usually called the president
rhizomes	creeping stems that grow underground horizontally, sending out shoots above and roots below
rotis	Indian breads of any kind
shrine	a place or object which has a holy association
tsunamis	destructive waves which occur when the ocean's water is displaced by an earthquake

Index